UNCERTAIN
MYTHOLOGIES

UNCERTAIN MYTHOLOGIES

poems

JAMES ALAN RILEY

Shadelandhouse
MODERN PRESS

LEXINGTON, KENTUCKY

A Shadelandhouse Modern Press book
Uncertain Mythologies
poems
Copyright © 2024, Text and cover art by James Alan Riley
All rights reserved.

For information about permission to reproduce selections from this book,
please direct inquiries to permissions@smpbooks.com, or
Permissions
Shadelandhouse Modern Press, LLC
P.O. Box 910913
Lexington, KY 40591

Published in the United States of America by:
Shadelandhouse Modern Press, LLC
Lexington, Kentucky
smpbooks.com
Printed in the United States of America
First edition 2024
Shadelandhouse, Shadelandhouse Modern Press,
and the logo are trademarks of Shadelandhouse Modern Press, LLC.

ISBN: 978-1-945049-40-8
Library of Congress Control Number: 2024931551
Cover Art: *The Road* (oil on canvas, 22" x 28") by James Alan Riley
Cover Art Photograph of *The Road*: Mark Hackworth
Author photo: Tammy Riley

Cover and book design: iota books

for Tammy

CONTENTS

I.

The Visit | 1

Photograph | 2

Vista Cruiser | 3

The Second Day of Swimming Lessons | 4

A Memo from the Premonitions Bureau | 5

Theme Drinking on My Mother's Porch | 6

Limelight Hydrangeas | 7

My Eighty-Year-Old Mother Rides the Mechanical Bull at Hillbilly Days | 8

Still Life with Roses | 10

November Leaves | 11

The Last Time I Took Mom to Walmart | 12

The Knockout Roses Are Blooming | 14

Absence | 15

Flower Garden | 16

Harmony | 17

The River | 18

Grief As a Body of Water | 19

II.

Uncertain Mythologies | 25

How the Days Catch Us | 26

Most People Who Have Been Through What I've Been Through Are Dead | 27

Pentimento | 29

This is Not a Love Poem | 30

Journey | 31

Mira gestorum | 32

Piano Lessons | 33

Six Suites for Unaccompanied Cello | 34

Pareidolia | 37

Pink Floyd on a Bicycle | 38

Jazz Club Serenade | 40

The Bear on the Railroad Track | 41

The Dirt Bike | 42

Before the Pandemic | 43

Hansel and Gretel | 45

The Murder Hornets Are Coming! | 47

Violence Erupts at the Intersection of Parallel Universes | 49

Escape Mutations | 51

After the Pandemic | 52

From the Labyrinth of Lost Things | 53

III.

The Random Thoughts of an Old Man at the Turn of a New Century | 57

Dumb Things to Do After Thirty | 58

The War's Over, Grandpa | 59

Fata Morgana | 60

Dancing in the House of Marley | 61

The Tooth Fairy Deals with Inflation in the Same Way as the Rest of Us | 63

Binging *Naked and Afraid* | 64

Bullwinkle's Hat Trick #3 | 66

Not Like Old Westerns | 68

To the Pitcher, Having Lost His Arm | 69

Memories | 70

Turning Right | 71

Requiem | 72

Apologia | 73

Why Old Men Don't Write Poetry | 74

How to Leave a Room | 75

Planting the Trees | 76

Acknowledgments | 79

About the Author | 80

THE VISIT

I am sleeping on a pallet
in the living room, the blue
pilot light from the gas furnace
flickering beneath the floor,
the metal grate hot to the touch.

My mother and her mother
are sitting beneath the soft light
from a lamp on the kitchen table,
their voices hushed, whispering
in strange melodies the sense
of who I am in this house.

PHOTOGRAPH

My grandfather leans against a fence
with a hammer in his hand.
He is smiling for a child
taking pictures with a toy camera.
The child does not understand
what is happening but the old man does.
He knows without looking over his shoulder.

He is wearing a long-sleeved shirt
in the heat of summer, attaching
a loose strand of barbed wire
to a split rail fence. The house
in the background is painted white,
the barn filled with hay as he pauses
to have his picture taken,
his white hair tangled,
his free hand resting on the post.

I did not realize what was happening
when he raised his hand to shade his eyes
from the sun, the barn overgrown
with bunch grass and tangled briars,
the stone foundation of the house unloosed
from the ground. Such wingless creatures
have no agenda but to come undone,
pushing their small stones in search
of lost causes.

VISTA CRUISER

We knew there was a heaven in those days
because we could see it through the tinted
windows above the second row of seats
where the argument over who would sit where
didn't stop until Daddy pulled the Vista Cruiser
to the side of the road and said
the next one to complain would get
their britches warmed, the five of us
convinced he meant every word as we drove
forty miles on some winding back highway
to the only Catholic church within an hour's drive.

The road to salvation was paved in those days
by the threat of my father's belt,
my mother saying you kids mind your father.
He sat in the car with the windows down
during Mass, listening to the radio
and my sister's version of "Blowing in the Wind"
from the back, jacked up on the Dramamine
we all had to take until Mom realized
it was only her youngest who suffered
motion sickness, the rest of us sympathy puking.

"Mom" was all my sister had to say
and the car would come sliding to a stop
on the shoulder of the road, doors opening
on the passenger's side so our new Vista Cruiser
wouldn't smell like our old blue Chevy smelled
since that day on our way back from first Communion
when five little Catholic kids full of sugar
cookies and fruit punch proved to my father
there was but one God.

THE SECOND DAY OF SWIMMING LESSONS

Standing at the edge of the city pool
with a handful of other five-year-olds,
I waited on my first day of swimming lessons
not knowing what to expect but prepared
by weeks of prompting from my mother
who assured me swimming was not only fun
but necessary for survival, never mind
the blood at the bottom of the pool
blossoming like a dark flower.

One of the lifeguards had dived too deep
and knocked himself unconscious.
He lay drowning at the bottom of the pool,
his limp body face down in the deep end
while the other lifeguards screamed
and worked to get him out of the water.
They laid him on his stomach and pumped
water from his mouth, blood pouring
from an open gash on his forehead.
He hadn't moved when they covered him
to the neck with a sheet and loaded him
on a stretcher and lifted him
into the back of an ambulance.

The next day, there was only me and one
other kid whose mother was obsessed
with the fear it would be her child
drowned from not learning to swim.
"There's nothing to be afraid of,"
Mom said, "Just close your eyes."
But I couldn't do it, having begun
to suspect the rumors were true.

A MEMO FROM THE PREMONITIONS BUREAU

While you were sleeping, a comet
appeared beneath the southern tip
of Ursa Major. It will only be visible
to the naked eye for a few days.
Make no mistake, there will be regrettable
decisions made in the coming years.

While you were washing dishes,
a tornado was brewing on the plains
that would grow in size and strength
over the next forty-eight hours.
There is sometimes a reason to leave
the dirty dishes in the sink.

Had you thought the answer was yes,
you might have stopped rather than gone
about your day and watched the clouds
gather like fog along the ridge.
Did you spend your time wisely?

When the thought occurred to you
that this moment might come
whether you were prepared or not,
the bees on the hydrangeas outside
your bedroom window were skipping
from blossom to blossom like assassins.

THEME DRINKING ON MY MOTHER'S PORCH

In her later years, my mother would only drink
when I came to visit, which meant twice a year
we felt obligated to make up for lost time,
theme drinking on her porch of an evening
as the sky turned dark and the stars appeared.
We had Jim Beam and Coke night, then cosmopolitans.
Margarita night was always a favorite, sitting up
long past sobriety and laughing like children,
the rim of our stemmed glasses heavily salted.

Most of our discussions were philosophical.
We talked about the past and the nature of loss,
the grief we went through when Daddy died
and then my older brother, how the world
had never been the same after they were gone.
We didn't solve the world's problems
but that doesn't mean we didn't try,
arguing religion and championship wrestling
as if they were the same, though one was obviously fake.
We talked about the book on gardening my grandfather
wrote by candlelight during the Great Depression.

"Your daddy never cared much for your grandpa,"
Mom said. "He thought your grandpa was a know-it-all
and he was, but then so was your daddy."

The most important question we asked was never
about the past but the immediate future.
Should we make another drink or be sensible
and go to bed? Turns out we grew less sensible
as the night passed, having learned it didn't matter
which subject we chose to discuss, our conclusions
were always the same, the night sky filled with stars.

LIMELIGHT HYDRANGEAS

The hydrangeas are blooming
beneath the illusion of afternoon sun,
the uneven lines and depth of shadow
deceiving in the slow motion of light.
The blossoms breathe this empty house
its dark rooms where time passes
without notice, where yellow and red
and blue make gray, a window shade
the color of human skin. Does it matter
these scars have been cut with a blade,
revisions in a world where more paint
is the solution to every mistake,
our brief disappointments hidden
beneath layers of random color,
the dark ground, the open sky.

We cannot deny what has come before,
having seen with certainty each stroke.
Hope is cerulean blue, yellow ocher
the present tense. We have come to a place
where each word has been carved with a knife,
the curtains drawn, the desire to push
these colors into shapes that suggest comfort.
Do not ask who lived in this house,
the shadows add depth to the light,
the last stroke of blue a sigh of relief
though the technique is flawed, the search
left wanting beneath a wash of limelight.

MY EIGHTY-YEAR-OLD MOTHER RIDES
THE MECHANICAL BULL AT HILLBILLY DAYS

On the third weekend in April, rain or shine,
the hillbillies descend on Pikeville, Kentucky,
with their bib overalls and mason jars of moonshine,
the streets closed to traffic and lined on both sides
with food trucks that offer everything fried,
Oreos and sticks of butter, elephant ears.
Locals and out-of-towners stroll from the carnival
to the gazebo in the city park, continuous bluegrass
rising from a makeshift stage outside the courthouse,
"Rocky Top" from a loudspeaker that distorts each version
beyond recognition, the wail of a banjo and fiddle
the backdrop to countless booths of vendors
selling statues of coal miners carved from coal,
old-timey pop guns and homemade jewelry fashioned
from river glass, nickel made to shine like silver.

My mother ate a funnel cake with powdered sugar,
said the food was worth the fourteen-hour drive
from Tulsa, not to mention the atmosphere.
She was having the time of her life.
There were booths where you could throw an ax
or break a glass beer bottle with a baseball bat.
People were paying good money to bungee jump
from a crane in the movie theater parking lot
until the city shut them down for being fools.
The local candidate for jailer had fashioned
a makeshift jail from PVC pipes painted black
to make it look like you were behind bars
while having your picture taken in handcuffs
and an orange-striped jail shirt.

We watched the mechanical bull throw people
to the ground, mostly young men with nothing
better to do and even less to lose,
their girlfriends poured into cut-off jeans
like ten pounds of sugar in a five-pound sack.

"You want to ride that thing, don't you?" I said.
I knew the answer before I asked.
"Hold my bourbon and Coke," Mom said.

It took three of us to get her in the saddle
where she sat teetering on the brute machine.
"Hold on," I said before taking her picture,
the open palm of her hand waving.

STILL LIFE WITH ROSES

I have waited too long to prune
the roses in her winter garden,
stepping from the porch with my shears,
my hands cold in their cotton gloves.

When the blossoms were full
and splayed in wild shades of red
across the wide expanse of the yard,
we sat on the porch together
ignoring the faded color of the blooms
we cut and carried in the house.

NOVEMBER LEAVES

My mother answers the phone.
The November leaves are falling.
She looks out her kitchen window,
sips her margarita and laughs.

She doesn't care about the leaves.
She knows until the trees are bare,
there is nothing she can do but wait,
make herself comfortable.

When she fell and broke her hip,
the doctor said the bone probably broke
before she fell and not the other way around.
"This is where we are," he said.

Only later did I realize he meant
we were waiting for the last
of the leaves to fall, the bare trees
singing where we are going
rather than where we've been.

THE LAST TIME I TOOK MOM TO WALMART

Too weak to walk on her own,
she sat in the wheelchair
with an open bag of diapers
in her lap. We had come
to return the diapers
but she wanted to look
at women's clothes first

so we took our time, moving
down long rows of brightly
colored skirts and blouses,
aisles of pastel sweaters.
She touched each piece,
measuring its texture
with the tips of her fingers.

When we got to customer service,
she set the bag of diapers
on the counter and told the woman
she needed a smaller size.

"I'm sorry," the woman said,
"but you can't return these.
They've been opened."

"I know that," Mom said.
"I'm the one who opened them."

"I'm sorry," the woman said,
"but it's store policy."

I'm not sure Mom understood
what store policy had to do
with being eighty years old,
confined to a wheelchair
and needing diapers.

"Could I please speak," she said,
"to someone smarter than you?"

THE KNOCKOUT ROSES ARE BLOOMING

The knockout roses are blooming
in red bursts out her window.
They are the color of lost causes.

My mother reaches for me
with one hand, holds my wrist.
"I don't like it here," she says.

There is a pause between each word
as she gathers her thoughts,
searching. "I want, I want to—"

I know what she is trying to say.
She asks the same question each visit.
"–come with you," she says.

I sit and hold my mother's hand.
Outside her window, the knockout roses
are blooming the color of lost causes.

ABSENCE

My mother's voice calling
me to come inside, my name
in a burst of fallen leaves

as the wind pushes its way
through the winter trees
crows rise from the ridge

the sky fills with wild
tangents of flight blown
like scraps of paper

above the rush of all that color,
their call caught in the same
unloosed motion as the leaves

FLOWER GARDEN

The saddest memories
always bloom first,
the heart-shaped flower
of your mother's smile
among the scarlet tips
of the early tulips.
The hyacinths along
the walkway blossom
beneath a dogwood tree,
the pierced sacrament
of white crosses
reminiscent of some other
passion, their grief
concealed by a cluster
of jonquils, marigolds
and orangewood poppies
whose black eyes stare
in silence from raised
beds of gray stone
where the forget-me-nots
tremble, rising from their
terra cotta pots to sing.

HARMONY

comes always in a minor key
played adagio with strings,
the slow rumble of percussion
in the distance rising
from a brass fermata
that demonstrates control
for a short duration only

comes in the third movement
after the crescendo of desire
has faded, the unexpected bridge
with its realization that time
is measured by the illusion
of time when there is no illusion,
the final recognition followed
always by regret

comes in a coda that returns
at the end to the song
we were playing before
the orchestra arrived
and, ordered in their seats,
began in unison to follow
the conductor's dancing baton.

THE RIVER

I was on the phone
with my sister
when my mother died.
I could hear
her labored breath
in the background,
my sister crying
she didn't know
what to do.

"I have to go," she said.

When she called back,
there was only silence
in the background,
her words a river
of strange melodies
rising from the distance
between us.

GRIEF AS A BODY OF WATER

Depth is not the problem
once you're in over your head.
The hillside behind the house
reaches for an empty sky,
one hand outstretched
from the shadow of bare trees.

There is the sound of water
coming down the mountain
and the sound of heavy rain.
Cars pass in slow waves
on the highway in the distance.
You can get too close to some things
to see them clearly for what they are.
More people drown in their own bathtub
than get swept out to sea by the tide.

*

Most bodies of water appear calm
on the surface, contemplative,
the dark hills in the distance,
the quiet reflection of trees
tapping you on the shoulder as if to say
You are not where you're supposed to be,
sitting in an empty room for twenty minutes
wondering why no one else came to the meeting.

Drifting to sleep that night,
you realize you were the only one
who was in the wrong place at the wrong time,
that your meeting went on without you,
never mind it took you all day
to realize your mistake.

    *

We sometimes find ourselves
in strange and unexpected places,
confused by the ambient light,
the weight of water in our hands.
What did you think was going to happen?
That you could see through all that water?
That the opposite of rising to the surface
was not sinking to the muddy bottom?

The answer is always the same.
Depth is not the problem
once you're in over your head.
The problem is one of proximity,
of being too close to see clearly
what is right before your eyes,
the open palm of your hand,
the sound of your voice calling.

    *

The only motion is the motion of silence,
the only green the stick thistle and weeds
you should have cut but didn't.
You should have cleared the brush
from the foundation of the house.

You sit at the window and watch the rain.
A slow drizzle soaks the patio and dead grass
beneath the jagged stems of the winter roses.
Brown leaves are matted to the sidewalk,
the hydrangeas cut to the ground.

*

Floating is the last sensation,
the pain numbed by morphine
in steadily increasing doses.
You can get too close to some things
and not realize your mistake,
sitting alone in an empty room,
thinking you're getting better.
I don't know what else to say.
How could you come to this moment
and not be prepared for its coming,
the surrounding hills a body of water.

UNCERTAIN MYTHOLOGIES

The mimosa tree beside the house
is blooming, the hummingbirds ecstatic,
drifting from blossom to blossom
in random patterns of pink lace.
I watch them from the yard
as they dart from flower to flower,
hovering motionless as their wings
vanish, their frail bodies balanced
on air as they tilt toward the shadows
and disappear. One stops as I watch,
resting on the thinnest of moments
before resuming its pirouette
of random short flights
through the branches of the tree.

Some mysteries cannot be measured.
Their wings beat eighty times
per second though the math
is exponential as they travel
from Guadalajara to Veracruz
before returning to the mimosa
in the yard beside my house
on the same day each year.

There is no mythology
for such wild harmonies,
the sun already risen, the moon,
stopping only when I turn to look,
lingering just long enough to admire
these small birds moving in unison
from flower to pink flower,
their silent, unseen orbits tuned
to the rhythm of invisible wings.

HOW THE DAYS CATCH US

off guard with their sudden
persistent alarm, descending
sleep like a flight of stairs,
the day's appointments
answering the smell of coffee
with obligation, the birds
in their early surprise
asking where is this blue sky
on your list of days?

MOST PEOPLE WHO HAVE BEEN THROUGH WHAT I'VE BEEN THROUGH ARE DEAD

My wife says it's because I'm a rule breaker,
parking in the drive-through pick-up space
at Tudor's Biscuit World when I'm not picking
anything up from the drive-through.
"But I went through the drive-through,"
I say, "that should count for something,
and I'm eating their breakfast biscuit."
"But you aren't picking anything up,"
she says. "You already have your food."

There are three spaces for drive-through
pick-up at Tudor's Biscuit World.
The only one taken besides the one I'm in
was taken by some guy who went inside to eat.
"He's not picking anything up," I say.
"Another rule breaker," she says.
"Did you think you were the only one?"

The truth is I hadn't given it much thought,
but I do drive too fast on backroads
and I drive too slowly when I'm on the highway,
even, God forbid, when I'm in the fast lane.
I don't always move the furniture when I vacuum
and I sometimes move my ball in the rough.
The list goes on. I wear jeans with holes
in the knees and T-shirts with coffee stains.
I don't always comb my hair when I go out
in public, even when I'm going to Walmart.

The general consensus seems to be I'm a menace
to society, skirting the law every chance I get,
oblivious to how an organized society is supposed
to work, and I suppose it's true. I sometimes
take the long way when a shorter route exists,
and I rarely use my turn signal. I was pulled once
for this infraction and asked by a state trooper
outside Nashville, Tennessee, if I were transporting
large quantities of heroin or meth or substantial
amounts of cash. "I do have a lot of money,"
I was forced to admit, "three hundred and forty
dollars to be exact." The state trooper looked
at me like I'd misunderstood the question.
"Never mind," he said, "use your turn signal."

PENTIMENTO

Her perfume lingers in the bedroom,
the aroma of scented lotions and creams
long after she's gone to work.

She moves to the rhythm of absence,
standing at the mirror in silence,
the light from the window filling

the dark room with color, the whisper
of last night's promise echoing
all this next day, calling as if

she were standing at the door,
the luxury of so much color
in the soft folds of her hair.

THIS IS NOT A LOVE POEM

I watch her dress
each morning for work,
perfectly balanced
as she pulls her skirt
over her black panties
and buttons her blouse.
This is not a love poem.
She is dressing for work,
a blue pump on one foot,
a brown wedge on the other.
She asks a question impossible
to answer as she turns
from the mirror and lets
her hair fall to one side,
pulls it back and lets
it fall again from the memory
of her body inside her pencil
thin skirt and silk blouse,
her panties and black bra.
She has run three miles already
and rubbed lotion on her legs,
her foot resting on the edge
of the tub.

JOURNEY

from this dream of rivers
stretching into the distance

from these hills that surround
the house like the rim of a cup

from the last light of day
night falling from the water's edge

a whistle following this path
through the apple trees

the garden where a message
lies written in stone, beyond

reach, the gathering stars,
the slow motion of ground

beneath our feet as we walk
last night's dream

MIRA GESTORUM

The purgatory angels are singing,
their medieval voices floating
on the afternoon in harmony
with the cicadas, the drone
of tree frogs like wild-eyed monks,
the night bird's solfeggio.

PIANO LESSONS

Having never unlocked my right hand
from my left, I bang at the keys
and think but for the want of practice
would this come easily, scales
breaking tangents across an empty room,
a barrage of meaningless notes
echoing call and return, a sadness
I cannot unhear playing
when we were young and burning
to hear the song again, caught
in its wildly passing score.

SIX SUITES FOR UNACCOMPANIED CELLO

A single voice implies harmony,
the heart of our understanding
from this earth of flowing rhythms,
morning sun through our bedroom window,
bluebells in the yard, each call
in unison chanting *yes*
as if the motion of our bodies
could sing these lost memories
in quiet requiem to hear again
melodies abandon all language.

And do these moments provide solace?
The voice I hear calling my name,
various shades of turquois and blue,
the open white sky's reflection in water.
What else but a minor key
for a season we once held dear,
those we love calling from the shadows
gathered rising in the yard at night,
the soft glow of bone white moon
on grass through trees, through branches.
How could we not know that what we heard
might one day be understood as music?

Come outside and stand in the yard,
take my hand and follow me to the yard,
the warm descent of light rising,
whispering *yes* and promising *yes*
as this moment dances before our eyes,
our solace from want this motion swaying
to the implied harmony of bluebells,
a bouquet of cut flowers to carry inside,
these unloosed bodies no longer bound.

Take these elaborate voices,
intricate rhythms among the constant
     echo of solitary notes
sometimes forgotten but present,
surrounding our voices as we recall
what happened and how the days
      got away from us,
the nights warm beneath the blanket
of our longing for that same smooth
distance where we once slept,
leaving only the soft touch
of your body beneath the stroke
of my hand on your strings.

A song in the tall grass calls our name,
a song in the bare limbs of the trees
even as spring approaches. They sing
these yellow flowers whose name I forget,
the corporeal become the cosmic
beneath our feet as we walk this grief
      stricken ground,
our time together music that lingers
beyond the touch of your hand,
the sound of your voice.
Did they come to me in a dream?
Am I dreaming now or will the night
find me in your arms again and whisper
forget me forget me not, each petal
a gift we held and could not let go.

Forget me. Forget me not.
The words lie scattered
on the ground at our feet
though spring approaches,
the voice you hear my voice,
the hand you touch my hand.
I am waiting for you now,
even now as we watch evening
slip from the shadows
refusing to gather light
in the soft glistening
of the winter bluebells,
their small hands rising
from the ground, whispering
we are together we are together,
rhythm at the heart of our lives.

PAREIDOLIA

It is the songs we sing that divine us,
old recordings of barbershop quartets,
jazz band improvisations on a saxophone.
They are the dancing clouds above
those who survived by seeing the face
of a lion in the tall grass, fear
in the eyes of a cardboard box,
surprise from a kitschy blender.

What does it mean we find
significance in random designs,
meaning where there is no meaning?
A shaft of light in some grotto
and the pilgrims won't stop coming
to rattle their beads, trading bats
for butterflies, a fish stick Jesus
on a kaiser bun, a three cheese
thin crust Virgin Mary pizza.

PINK FLOYD ON A BICYCLE

If you don't know the story,
you should. Wait for the lion
to roar and on the third roar
turn down the volume on the tv
and start the album.

What you will find
may be pure synchronicity
but the coincidence of images
coinciding with the music
from *Dark Side of the Moon*
suggests something purposeful,
though madness often requires
its own unique purpose.

Enter Miss Almira Gulch
pedaling her bicycle
to the clang of bells
from the song "Time,"
arriving at Dorothy's farm
in search of her little dog
as one of the backup singers
in the studio whispers,
"If you can hear this,
you're dying."

Everything else is speculation
from a world forty years gone,
suggesting the real value lies
in turning up the volume
and riding through the open
countryside behind the house,

the tattered coops littered
with red roosters and hens,
chicken wire fences and sheds,
the gravel road winding
through farmhouses not unlike
the Gale homestead in a world
that no longer exists, Kansas
become Kentucky in one
continuous loop.

JAZZ CLUB SERENADE

I got a pack of saxophones
rolled in my T-shirt sleeve
patent leather downtown shoes
shining major tonic scale
I got a funny way of walking

I got a funky slide trombone
nine-pound hammer cello bone
I get lost sometimes in three-four time
the music from another room
hot plate in pocket state of mind

I got a wheelchair xylophone
crash helmet bebop monkey bone
violin string broken wing
hissing sidewalk kneecap snare
G minor train wreck in the skins

I got a reason to be gone
someplace I know I shouldn't go
I had a woman but she broke my heart
18 karat for a fling
I got a way of losing things

I got a case of can't go home
a little bourbon on the side
shot glass backlash broken wheel
crazy dark chop fractured vibe
it's not the meaning but the feel

THE BEAR ON THE RAILROAD TRACK

There was no bear
on the railroad track
but that didn't stop
people from leaning out
their balcony windows
for a better look,
pointing into the distance
as if imagining the one thing
they never expected to see
coming from the dark woods.

There was no bear
on the railroad track
but that didn't keep someone
from calling animal control
to report what they'd seen,
worried about seeing such a thing
come wandering from the woods,
paws scraping loose gravel.

There was no bear
on the railroad track
but there was a railroad track
and that made the bear
more believable for those
who saw its thick fur
with their own eyes.

THE DIRT BIKE

With some resignation
she tells the story again
at the boy's request,
how she was bragging
to her brother about
riding dirt bikes
as a child and knowing
how to ride a dirt bike.

"There she sits,"
her brother said.

We've all had those moments
when fate or destiny comes
together to work against
our mostly logical selves,
suggesting we do something
we might otherwise never consider,
the motor roaring as the handlebars
rose up before her and crashed
headlong into a wall, the bike
falling on her leg as she climbed
from beneath another bad decision
and left snubbing for the house.

The boy finds this story hysterical
and asks to hear it again, though
after a while the meaning has changed,
the dirt bike become something more
than the dirt bike we remember.

BEFORE THE PANDEMIC

We stopped on Bourbon Street
to have our picture taken,
smiling at a passing stranger
holding my wife's phone.

We had come from the Red Fish Grill,
a plate of oysters Beinville
and glass of house merlot,
though my wife doesn't care
for oysters or drink alcohol.

This was in February.
We had heard of the virus in Wuhan,
that there might be a case in Washington,
but that's about all we knew other than
it was contagious and might spread.

After smiling for the camera,
we toured St. Louis Cemetery No. 1,
the oldest cemetery in New Orleans
where the famous voodoo queen Marie Laveau
lay buried for over a century,
her tomb a mausoleum above ground,
the concrete cracked and weathered
and covered with hand drawn *XX*'s.

"Do not to touch anything," our guide said.
"Do not carry stones home in your pocket
 to disprove the curse. We get them back
 all the time in the mail."

I suppose we should have known better,
strolling the French Market no longer
in search of souvenirs, listening
to a jazz ensemble, the drum
of street vendors on empty buckets.

HANSEL AND GRETEL

It was the dream of herd immunity
they sought, holding a tattered map
beneath the lamp in search of crumbs
to lead them away from this gingerbread
house where the stench of burning hair
and cries from those most vulnerable
were surrounded by silence and risk.

Their ignorance may be legend
but they have an *ethos* for survival,
the light shimmering umber and ochre
in the distance, the heat rising
from these dark woods that hold
the past like a child by the hand.

It's not the threat so much
as the discomfort for most,
the thought of restricted travel
as if there were a plentitude
of better choices scattered
behind each step, six feet
being the measure of most graves,
the commitment and casual glance
beneath this canopy of candy
where the young continue to party,
a jar full of juju beans to the first
diagnosed from those attending.

Fun for the young and the young at heart,
their tattoos a parchment of skulls
for those who don't believe in masks,
dousing the fire and tramping the wet ashes
from the front parlor to the back room

where the oven is still warm to the touch,
where unsavory events are recorded in real time
by those with nothing to lose. Listen!
The celebration has begun but the balloons
at the party are black balloons rising
from the torn scraps of a leather scroll
like the raised voices of children
singing in unison, their open mouths
pronouncing the future a dark wave.

THE MURDER HORNETS ARE COMING!

What pandemic worth its death rate
doesn't include a good plague?
Did you think all those stories
in the Bible were fiction?
I've got some bad news for you if you did.
There was some creative non-fiction included
and a handful of personal essays,
most of which ended badly.

No end of the world
would be complete without a swarm
of killer insects moving in next door
like a family of crackheads with a flatbed
trailer behind their truck, playing
their music too loud at night and junking
up their yard with empty beer cans.

It's only a matter of time
before they're knocking on your door,
asking for a ride to the Dollar General
or to borrow twenty bucks so they can pay
their electric bill, only you know
they're not going to pay their electric bill.
They're murder hornets. They're going
straight to the Speedway for lottery tickets
and an eighteen-pack of beer in cans.

The police won't be able to do anything
with them. You're going to be waking up
in the middle of the night for the rest
of this pandemic, wondering what that noise
is you keep hearing only to realize
the murder hornets are partying in your yard,

high on homebrew meth and who knows what else,
singing "Free Bird" at the top of their lungs
and revving up their junker cars.

"Would you fucking murder hornets
go to bed," you want to yell
out the bedroom window, but you know
it won't do any good. Murder hornets
don't know when to go to bed.
They don't know how to behave,
flying around biting the heads off
honeybees just for kicks, getting
arrested and taken to jail
only to get out the next day.
It's going to be hard getting through
this pandemic without a cigarette.

VIOLENCE ERUPTS AT THE INTERSECTION OF PARALLEL UNIVERSES

Let me start by suggesting
the plumber was subpar,
leaving a hole in the floor
the size of a laundry basket
beneath the kitchen sink.
He didn't finish the job
and now something was bumping
through the dark house
in the middle of the night.

I got a hammer for self-defense
and followed the sound to the kitchen
where I found a possum sitting
on top of my icebox, a big possum,
fat and white-faced and staring
at the hammer in my hand
like the next move was mine.

Only I didn't have a next move
and before I could think of one,
he hissed at me, jumped to the floor
and ran behind the stove.
I grabbed his tail just before
it disappeared and carried
him twisting to the door,
clawing and biting at my hand
to get loose. I know, right?
Three in the morning, half asleep
and under attack in my own kitchen.

I did the only thing I could think
to do. I hit him with the hammer,
not a glancing blow, and then I hit him
again. It was the second blow that got
his attention. He calmed down after that
and stayed calm until I tossed him
out in the yard where he hit with a thud
and sat on the sidewalk shaking his head.
I don't think he knew any more about
what just happened than I did, looking
around like he was seeing everything
for the first time.

ESCAPE MUTATIONS

The language of science always catches me
off guard, the viral threat of what it means
exactly that the mutants have escaped.

I imagine them scaling a chain-link fence,
throwing blankets over razor wire
and disappearing into the night

like serial killers with homemade shivs.
Should I nail my windows shut?
Should I fix my doors with locks?

I have a gun but it's not loaded,
and the word is you won't recognize them
when they come, which complicates things.

Your average mutant's prime mechanism
for avoiding detection is disguise,
their very existence predicated
on not being recognized as a threat.

AFTER THE PANDEMIC

It was a little rough at first
on the house pets and the farm animals
who depended on us for their daily bread,
the pigeons in the park, for instance,
the rats accustomed to piles of garbage.

The animals in the zoo didn't fare
too well, though after the initial shock
wore off, things got better.
The rats went back to being rats,
happily fending for themselves.
The pigeons did fine without statues.

And then the grasses took root.
The vines and weeds tore everything
to the ground one brick at a time.
Iron bridges rusted and collapsed,
concrete buildings crumbled until,
after only a few thousand years,
Mount Rushmore and the Great Wall
of China were all that was left,
though there was no one to explain
the expression on those worn faces,
or where, on that other overgrown continent,
an emperor's militia once stood
to defend the civilized world
from the onslaught of Mongol hordes.

FROM THE LABYRINTH OF LOST THINGS

The present tense is a violent season,
dashcam footage of a body in the street,
a man face down on the sidewalk.
Social media blogs record automatic gunfire
behind a stone wall, a car being pulled
from the lake. There is always blood
on the knife when the crops fail.

Found things often appear mysterious
out of context, the palm of my hand
holding a coin, a pack of cigarettes
in the kitchen drawer. Reality
is only metaphor in hindsight.
I have been down this road before.
I know all my scenes by heart
though I sometimes find myself
in strange and unexpected places,
the sky filled with the motion of leaves,
the tilt of evening.

The fittest of bodies found
had well-groomed fingernails
and perfumed hair, a stomach
full of cereals and milk,
vegetables. Those responsible
were both gracious and efficient,
the four bronze mounts of his leather
armband mostly ceremonial, though
he did not tie his own hands
behind his back nor suffer
the axe alone before disappearing
into the next two thousand years.

THE RANDOM THOUGHTS OF AN OLD MAN
AT THE TURN OF A NEW CENTURY

Facts rise from the handwritten
note in the seat beside me
as I wait for the light to change,
broccoli and brussels sprouts,
a merlot the color of bruise.
There is meaning if you look
but there is not always meaning,
a body found in the ditch
beside the road brutalized
by some handsome monster smiling
wicked innocence in bas-relief,
smoking with his kids in the car.

I have lost the ability
to tell which is worse,
the looking or the looking away
as I sit among the silhouettes,
their faces turned to their phones,
their eyes strange hieroglyphs
that prove only what was once true
false.

They are telling me something
I already know, misinformation
appearing in the strangest of places,
on bumper stickers and highway signs,
the deadpan social media snark
as shadows rise from the ironweed
at the Walmart intersection,
a child's shoe hidden in the grass.

DUMB THINGS TO DO AFTER THIRTY

I'm not sure I need a hover board.
That might change but for now
I'm good. I have a pair of in-line
skates in the garage beside
an unused pair of roller skates,
number five on the list of dumb things
to do after you turn thirty.

I turned thirty a long time ago.
I'm sixty-six as I sit here
this morning drinking coffee
and I have a long list of things
I won't be doing for reasons
based mostly on self-preservation.
Forget rock climbing, I don't climb
stairs without one free hand in case
I lose my balance or my knees give.
Sky diving. Hang gliding. Base jumping.
Not likely. Some days just getting
my pants on in the morning without
catching my toe is a challenge.

THE WAR'S OVER, GRANDPA

This is me cleaning
the refrigerator
because the kitchen stinks
when I open the door.
I throw everything out
that has even the slightest
potential to stink,
smoked turkey sandwich meat,
pizza boxes and half-empty
cartons of cottage cheese,
bacon dated in geological time.

This is me throwing
everything away,
the eighteen almost empty
low-fat salad dressings
in the door, the empty jar
of mayonnaise behind the leftover
McDonald's bag and all those
little ketchup, mustard
and sweet relish packets
that have accumulated
over the years from various
fast-food restaurants.

FATA MORGANA

I was driving Kaden to school
when we came around a curve
on Ratliff's Creek and found
a rafter of wild turkeys jagged
and scattering in the road.

There were so many we had to stop
and wait, the gangly birds jerking
up the hillside in bursts of flight
before vanishing in the underbrush.

DANCING IN THE HOUSE OF MARLEY

When we took the grandkids to Florida
that summer, we committed to being a family
in full-on tourist mode, khaki shorts,
matching loud shirts just crazy enough
for two teenage boys to think cool
even after the word *cool* had been designated
a grandpa thing. All bets were off
at the table in back, the thump
of a bass guitar echoing on the downbeat
from speakers big as ice boxes hidden
behind black crosses on a field of green.

I was watching you read the menu
across the table, the boys joking
Bob was one of Grandpa's Rasta friends,
surrounded by photographs of a smiling
Bob Marley hanging from the stucco walls,
his expression strangely appropriate
in the context of moments we won't forget.

I don't know what I was thinking.
It's not something you feel coming
until you're on your feet, dancing
a mostly grandpa version of some rogue
boogie-woogie gone jerky in every way
jerky can be understood as a negative
description of dancing.

The chopped and awkward rhythm
made the presentation worse,
an unsyncopated two-step shuffle
of mostly old-men nonsense. I recall
a kind of mash potato thing going on

with my arms and Kaden laughing
in two octaves, Colby too embarrassed
to watch, his face in his hands.
The unexpected had taken us to a place
we might otherwise have never found
and I knew at the time we would remember
the moment not for what it was
but for what it would become.

**THE TOOTH FAIRY DEALS WITH INFLATION
IN THE SAME WAY AS THE REST OF US**

How do I explain the look
on my granddaughter's face
when she smiles to show me
her missing tooth?

"Did the tooth fairy leave
a dime under your pillow?"
I ask, underestimating
in the way of all things Grandpa
the value of even our myths.

She looked a little confused
at first, doing the math in her head.
"Grandpa," she said, "five dollars."

BINGING *NAKED AND AFRAID*

It's not that I expected to find
a caiman in my yard, having
swum its way up the left fork
of the Big Sandy River from Peru
or Nicaragua or El Salvador.
We don't have caiman in this part
of Kentucky nor fer-de-lance coiled
motionless among the fallen palms
of some swamp bayou nightmare.

When I first thought *what am I
going to do about all these ants
in my kitchen*, it never occurred
to me that how they taste
might factor into my decision.
That same realization holds true
for the entire class of *Insecta*,
especially those in their larval form,
the yellow grubs and maggots
whose squirming bodies, packed
as they are with nutrients, do not
look edible even over an open fire.

It's a formula but it works
and it makes for good television,
though no naked human being is as tough
as they appear posing for a selfie
in a ghillie suit with an automatic
weapon strapped across their chest.
A machete with no blood on the blade
is not a real machete, and it doesn't
take a survivalist to start a fire
in the back yard with a gas grill.

The producers should address
the elephant in the Boma.
These naked bodies are not attractive.
That rhinoceros is not ready to charge.
His threatening posture is an illusion,
the jungle itself little more than camera
angles, alligators and B-roll spiders,
the human animal come to conquer
nature with nothing but a machete,
as if you could kill thousands
of mosquitoes with a machete
or bluff an infection once it enters
the bloodstream from contaminated water.
No wonder the howler monkeys
are losing their minds in the tops
of the tsin-tsin trees.

BULLWINKLE'S HAT TRICK #3

Unwholesome things do not normally appear
from hats, though that has not always been true.
Bullwinkle learned that lesson the hard way,
nothing up his sleeve, one hand vanishing
into a collapsible opera hat. What did he think
he was going to find? What might follow
an orangutan but a trumpeter swan?
The problem with pulling things from hats
is the odds never favor an empty hat.

Boris and Natasha were right about the failure
of their secret Goof Gas Gun, a cold-war cartoon
weapon designed to make everyone they shot stupid,
a weapon of mass destruction they fully intended
on using against the United States Congress,
only to realize, to their great dismay,
Goof Gas could not make something stupid
that was already stupid.

You think I'm making this up but I'm not,
the joke being once you reach a certain level
of dumb, there's no getting dumber,
a win/win in 1959 for Rocky and Bullwinkle.
Not so much for us these days. In the midst
of our own fractured fairy tale, dumber
may not only be possible but likely.
Stupid may be setting the bar too high
for even a healthy dose of Goof Gas.

Enter Bullwinkle J. Moose, thick-headed
magician extraordinaire, a little dim-witted
for a know-it-all but seemingly well-intentioned,
his gloved hand searching to the shoulder

for some presentable myth to explain how
things could have gone so terribly wrong.
When you are expecting a white rabbit,
the last thing you want is a rhinoceros.
It sounds like a joke but it's not,
the cheap suit, the gaudy tie and surrounding
claque of hats. The truth is the best illusions
have nothing to do with momentary distractions,
the magic as exponential as the math.

NOT LIKE OLD WESTERNS

where the fist fights never
bruise and a good horse
is always waiting to be ridden
out of town at a gallop

where all the bullets fired
in the air rise and rise
into the flatland sky
as if unaffected by gravity

and beautiful women sing songs
of endless love in saloons
filled with outlaw desperados
and honky-tonk piano players

where good always shoots straight
before riding into the sunset
the black hats easy to recognize
face down in the dusty street

TO THE PITCHER, HAVING LOST HIS ARM

I was carrying a ladder up the stairs
to repair the ceiling in the bedroom.
The air conditioner in the attic
had been leaking, water pouring
to the bedroom floor, the ceiling
soaked and soggy and turning brown,
the spackle coming loose in big chunks.
I didn't feel pain, but I must have
twisted my wrist going up the stairs,
tweaked it, as they say, when something's
hurt but not officially injured.

I lay in bed that night dreaming
I was on a pitcher's mound.
The manager had come from the dugout
to discuss the off-target dirt balls
I had been throwing, my fastball slow
as a change of pace, the runners
advancing. I don't remember
if he motioned to his right arm
or his left as he took the ball
from my glove, signaling I was done
for the night.

MEMORIES

I tell people I lost them
in a bar fight, sucker punched
by some brute who didn't realize
I kept them all in the same sack.

As exciting as that may sound,
I was never in a bar fight.
I went to a biker bar once
but no one was fighting.

Another version goes
they were never mine to begin with.
I lifted them sleight of hand
from a much younger man,

though I never stole anything
from anyone, and my skill
with a deck of cards is limited,
some might say, even, poor.

I'm not sure what happened.
One minute they were whispering
in my ear, reminding me not to forget
something important, then not so much.

The more likely scenario
is I had a hole in my pocket
and lost them one at a time
without noticing.

TURNING RIGHT

The children
eating peaches
with plastic spoons
have forgotten
who you are, those
who hurt you or said
the wrong thing,
those who cared
for whatever reason,
love, necessity.

None of that matters now
or is worth the effort
because you only turn
right, each new journey
a circle leading
to where you were
when you left home
that first time
thinking you might
never return.

REQUIEM

I have not left you all this time
in the silence of my future absence,
a pause between each word before
the colors arrive, permanent red
and vermillion, the periwinkle's bloom.
May I follow you with my hand
resting on your shoulder?

I have not left you on this path
behind the house that smells
of summer rain and fallen leaves,
beyond the yard full of apple trees
where we raised the boys.
Did you sew these pieces of bone
to the sleeve of my tattered shirt?

APOLOGIA

The apple blossoms fall
in a swirl of fragrance,
scattering on a blanket
beside the house. We watch
the night sky shudder
in perfect harmony
with the stars, light
drifting through the leaves
with each breath.
The petals list and spin
in a downpour of motion,
time consumed with its own passing.

Ashes to ashes, my love,
truth lives in the present
though the past lingers,
a lie we sometimes tell ourselves
to escape the realization
that you must one day live
without me. I apologize in advance
for my hand on your heart,
for the sky falling with such regret,
our shadows ascending like dreams.

WHY OLD MEN DON'T WRITE POETRY

because the grass grows uncut
beneath the autumn white sky,
the roses fading beneath
the shimmer of so much light

because the leaves drift
without purpose from the hillside
behind the house, the jays
calling from the underbrush

because the lines in the bedroom
have grown inches in only months,
rising in one long wave toward
a road that leads away from the house

because yesterday is a suit
of old clothes, tattered and worn
to the threads as you fall
into evening's empty sleeve

HOW TO LEAVE A ROOM

by walking slowly backwards
for dramatic effect, keeping
a close eye on those with plans
for an after-party, should there
be such a thing as an after party

by ascending the stairs
though this is not recommended
unless you don't mind people
discussing in infinite detail
your poor comb-over and thin arms

unbeknownst to those debating
carpentry skills and current events
in somber tones, their *ethos* unchanged,
their varied belief systems founded
on the presence of load-bearing walls

with much fanfare and applause,
one hand parade-waving goodbye
to all those who have gathered
to witness, with decorum if not grace,
a departure in such grand fashion

without looking back,
without the fear of being alone
or of what lies ahead, the music
from the next room playing
who will miss you when you're gone?

PLANTING THE TREES

I sometimes find myself
waiting only to realize
I have forgotten what
I was waiting for.
Did I mow the grass?
Should I weed the roses?
I don't always know,
so I sit in my truck
and wait, trying to recall
why I came outside
in the first place
only to remember
I have come to plant
the trees, a dogwood
and a redbud, along
the property line
because you never know
who might one day
need a shady place
to spend the afternoon.

ACKNOWLEDGMENTS

I wish to thank the editors of the following publications in which some of the poems in this book appeared.

"Fata Morgana" appeared in *Calliope*, Fall, 2021.

"Jazz Club Serenade" appeared in *The American Journal of Poetry*, Vol. 10. Spring, 2021.

Uncertain Mythologies was completed with the generous support of the Kentucky Arts Council, the state arts agency, which provides Artist Rescue and Disaster Recovery Grants from the Kentucky General Assembly and the National Endowment for the Arts.

ABOUT THE AUTHOR

JAMES ALAN RILEY is the author of *Broken Frequencies, a book of poems* (Shadelandhouse Modern Press, 2019). He is the recipient of a National Endowment for the Arts Fellowship, a 2023 Artists Relief and Disaster Recovery Grant from the Kentucky Arts Council (funded by the Kentucky General Assembly and the National Endowment for the Arts), the 2020 Thomas and Lillie D. Chaffin Award for Excellence in Appalachian Literature, two Al Smith Fellowships from the Kentucky Arts Council, and an Individual Artists Fellowship from the Ohio Arts Council. He edited Kentucky *Voices: A Collection of Contemporary Kentucky Short Stories* (PC Press, 1999) and was the founding editor of *The Pikeville Review* (1988–1999). He is Professor Emeritus of English at the University of Pikeville where he taught creative writing for 35 years. He lives in Pikeville, Kentucky, with his wife Tammy and their grandson Kaden.

www.ingramcontent.com/pod-product-compliance
Lightning Source LLC
Chambersburg PA
CBHW060537080526
44586CB00012B/774